Six Legs Jazz Club

A Journey to Uncovering Your Best Life

Dick Cappon and John R. Christensen

ISBN 1-894439-13-9
Printed and bound in Canada

Design and production by
Creative Bound International Inc.
www.creativebound.com   1-800-287-8610

Wendy O'Keefe, Creative Director
Gail Baird, Managing Editor

Illustrations: cover, pages 17, 69 & 97, Tracy-Lynn Chisholm

Printing number 10 9 8 7 6 5 4 3 2 1

National Library of Canada Cataloguing in Publication

Cappon, Dick, 1933-
       Six Legs Jazz Club : a journey to uncovering your best life / Dick
Cappon and John R. Christensen.

ISBN 1-894439-13-9

       1. Self-actualization (Psychology) I. Christensen, John R. (John
Robert), 1942- II. Title.

BF637.S4C377 2003   158.1   C2003-906270-8

Acknowledgments

Writing a book is many planets away from *wanting* to write a book! The process can be lonely, arduous, humbling, exhilarating, a confidence builder, judge and jury. What is most challenging of all is acknowledging those persons in our lives who have moved us to the point of actually completing the project.

To you, our supporters, family members and friends, may we simply and genuinely say, thank you and bless you. Your support and encouragement is acknowledged by our gift to you in each page of this book.

Contents

It is a late night, punctuating an exhausting week. The small twin-engine commuter plane banks to queue up in a holding pattern for landing. The black sky unveils a glorious carpet of sparkling lights pincushioning the ground. The aircraft shudders. It feels like a gentle shove, the kind expressed when someone accidentally bumps into you. A spit of flame shoots out from under the exhaust flap, then another and another, until the engine cowling is engulfed in a raging fireball.

The news flies among the passengers, giving rise to panic throughout the cabin. The pilot kills the engine, and the aircraft begins to descend in haste as the fire eats away at the wing. Your mind becomes fixated on the wild glow…and then there's just you alone, observing your thoughts. *Can this really be the end for me?* Your mind is crowded with the emotions of being mortal, of being in a die-able state. Mirrored through the window of the aircraft is your own hopeless face.

Preface to a Journey

The law of nature decrees that everything in life is constantly in the process of becoming something else. We are a part of that process whether we like it or not. We wake up every morning staring the future in the face, and use our day to burn through time and energy in the pursuit of our own busyness. When the end does come, have we used our time and energy wisely?

Our brains don't come with an instruction booklet. In today's fast-forward environment we seem to make it up as we go along. Life in the dominant culture seems a frantic rush into the unknown where we are constantly consuming more than we can absorb. We're into information overload, the consequences of which narrow our intelligence. This torrent of data separates us from our sense of self—and robs us of our memory of who we are.

Managing life is an evolving process. We are part of nature's evolution and are not meant to start from scratch. Humans are born with an emotional investment in themselves from which springs the yearning to create their own meaning to ensure their place in the world. Life is to be continued. We are here to learn, to build on and to grow out of the wisdom and lessons gleaned from our past. We're here to become more than we are at present.

The collection of personal wisdom can be a formidable task for any individual in a world that focuses on and covets only what is in front of us. Knowledge about ourselves isn't hard to find, it's just that most of us haven't looked. Our past sits waiting as information or data. Wisdom is derived from distilling the past and learning from it. Turning that data into self-knowledge and personal wisdom requires us to sift through and ponder our experiences, failures and successes to find the meaning of our life. If we are to live a life of confidence and focus, developing and growing into our full potential requires that we be true to those feelings and values that make up our unique self.

For co-author Dick Cappon, the beginnings of this book started years ago, gradually taking shape on each of his many flights around the world on business. From an airplane window, you see the world much differently than at ground level. You remove the strictures and boundaries that define life by the minute. Strapped in a seat at 35,000 feet, your mind's eye examines life from a different altitude. Doodles on a napkin began to give substance to reflections. They become the voice of your inner self. Questions appear from out of the blue, urging you to think about the path, the choices made in your life that now cause you to be sitting here. *Should I be here? Am I where I should be in my life?*

A life-altering event in co-author John Christensen's life began when he took a sabbatical from his coaching and consulting business to drive a big rig across North America. Driving a truck is a lonely life. Along the way, John kept a journal of his thoughts. The questions that streamed through John's thoughts were similar to the ones that confronted Dick. The epiphany is that it's important for all of us to take the time to catch up to ourselves. Whether you're winging your way through the clouds or whether your feet are planted firmly on the ground, stop and think what your life is all about. It's a liberating experience.

Getting the Future You Want From the Life You've Got

The true cost of living today is the high price we pay for losing ourselves in the swirl of a demanding life. When we lose our bearings, we end up in the middle of a maze. This book is for those individuals who have decided it is time to put passion and joy back into the creation of your life and work. We define breakthrough life strategies used by high achievers to manage their personal and work life with greater meaning, clarity and success. The "Six Legs" strategy is built around a series of probing questions designed to reconnect you with your unique self. Your answers will point the way to a more focused and meaningful future.

One flaw we all suffer is our ignorance of who we are. The Six Legs strategies presented here are a powerful investment in your future. The process is easy to digest. Embedded within its core are the techniques of using silence, reflection and personal doodles to uncover your expertise and self-knowledge. For, as author Charles Foster states, "you are the leading expert on your life."

Wally Amos, founder of Uncle Wally's Muffin Company and an acclaimed inspirational speaker and author, has become acutely aware of how life-changing experience has allowed him to arrive at a much better place in life. In his book *The Famous Amos Story*, Amos encourages his readers to take time to create space to look at where they've been, where they're at and where they're going. He believes passionately that to review our life is to become clearly aware of the growing experiences we've all had. And out of this, among other good things, comes our surprise at how strong and resilient we are, and how much we've learned. "Life is never what it really seems," writes Amos. "It is always more." So for him, the bottom line is that, in time, you look forward to those bumps in the road and see that they are blessings in disguise. Remember you are growing through them.

We know that we're living longer and healthier, and to that extent, life doesn't, nor should it, roll up in a hammock and lose its purpose. When we are aware of what's behind us, the only thing that's really important is what's ahead. We can take a look at our past, and use some of the wisdom we have accumulated to help transport us into a more secure future. The Six Leg strategies are as important to persons in their mid-twenties as they are to those in their sixties and well beyond. These are strategies to transport anyone through the journeys of life circumstance.

The Six-Legged Stool

The Six Legs stand together to form a stool. When you sit on your six-legged stool, it acts as an anchor securing you to your own abilities and potential in every aspect of your life. Whenever life begins to pull, distract and tease you in different directions, like the current on a river, you can sit on your stool and be reminded of who and what you are. In times of stress and strain, the stool reminds you of your beliefs, values and talents, enabling you to make choices that are best for you. The stool has authority and presence.

As you transition through the "thoughtwork" exercises described at the end of each chapter, you will begin to clarify the puzzle piece that is you—and where this piece fits in the jigsaw puzzle of life. As you journey through the Six Legs, you will build a greater awareness of just who you are. This is particularly key in the work component of your life. The more you understand of who you are and what makes you tick, the more focused you'll become on mapping your best future direction.

The first three legs of the stool will have you 'pull up a rock' and take personal inventory. These personal reflections will become a rich source of self-knowledge and wisdom, guiding you as you grow into yourself. The three legs surround the question "What's your B.A.G.?" Specifically, you will answer the questions "Where have I BEEN?" "Where am I AT?" and "Where am I GOING?" These questions surround the *being* of your life—how you have come to be who you are.

The last three legs of the stool will assist you in getting your A.C.T. together and show you how to feel great in your own skin. The three questions are "What have I ACCOMPLISHED?" "How did I CREATE what I did?" and "What were my personal TRIUMPHS?" These questions surround the *doing* of your life—how you did what you've done. You'll come out on the other side of the Six Legs process facing your future with confidence, clarity and focus.

Six Legs is about finding the "jazz" in your life. *Six Legs Jazz Club* will provide you with the tools and processes to uncover the composition of experiences, skills and passion that make you who you are—and the inspiration, confidence and eagerness to go after who you want to be.

The First Three Legs:

What's Your B.A.G.?

B.

The First Leg

Where Have I BEEN?

I have recently and reluctantly come to the conclusion that I am lost. Not just unsure that this is the right trail, but off any trail whatsoever. I find myself, figuratively, looking for footprints, broken twigs, any sign that someone has been over this ground ahead of me.

— as told to Bill Bridges, author and specialist in change management

The contorted rubber on Tara's Jag squealed in complaint as she whirled herself up the parking ramp, exiting the world headquarters of Quor Power International. The CEO muscled her way into Manhattan's frenzied traffic. The cell-phone jingled softly.

"I ate your chicken leg!" chuckled the muffled voice on the other end. Tara yanked out her hair clip releasing a cascade of lush, black hair. Her flashing green eyes darted into the traffic looking for a scant opportunity to barge her way into the line of overheated cars.

"Yeah, well I ate crow this afternoon at the executive meeting while Kyle shifted on the balls of his spine denying he was privy to the details on that Livingston deal," she responded, her ire rising.

"Tara," the voice responded, "Take a deep breath…maybe Kyle *wasn't* aware." Tara cut him off.

"He was aware all right. Two weeks ago at the management meeting, those same questions made him squirm. That's when I began to smell the truth. I just can't put my finger on why he declared himself in that meeting, and today when the issue came up, he suddenly feigned amnesia. He's a snake and I heard his tail rattling."

Lately Tara had begun to smell the truth about herself as well. Life was overwhelming. She was pushing so hard at advancing that she was losing control and leaving herself behind. There was lots of momentum, but little progress.

Deprived of Our Own Oxygen

The environment today requires us to be responsible for more, to do more with fewer resources, external assistance and guidance. We want decisions now, not tomorrow. We need information immediately. We don't have any breathing room; at least, that's how it seems. We have to keep gulping for air. We don't have time to breathe, to slow down, to step away from our spinning existence.

The reality is that we live along a superhighway of information technology, and the movement of life exceeds normal speed limits. At autobahn speeds, telephone poles zip by and blur as one. If someone were running alongside and tapped you on the shoulder to ask, "Excuse me, where are you going?" many of us would say "Don't bother me, I'm concentrating on going fast. Frankly, I'm expected to be doing a lot more and that's why I'm going so fast. I really don't have time to think about where I am going."

In his wonderful book entitled *Pebbles and Pearls*, author Jon Kabot-Zinn draws on a yoga tradition, describing the world as a spinning grindstone. We are either chewed up by it, or we can position ourselves to be honed like a blade.

Psychologist Carl Jung challenges us with the thought that at age fifty, life is done. Thereafter lies the quest for meaning. But our philosophy is that the quest begins when you have the ability to think, at whatever age. The quest for life's meaning is the most stimulating and seductive challenge to exercise the brain's neurons. The vehicle for questing is exploration and silent reflection. Taking time to reflect on who you are is thinking at its highest level. If you don't turn things over in your mind, to understand why you do things the way you do, you can become blind to your own nature. Life has no meaning until we think about it. Key insights and understandings of our life are hidden in the silence between our actions, words and thoughts. With the velocity of change today, the space of reflective silence has disappeared. Pondering and digesting your living history is a discipline involving self-imposed quiet time, in the form of mini-retreats or extended personal sabbaticals.

Silence Is Golden

The sound level of the world is getting louder. Most times we are not even conscious of the din going on around us. The noise is pervasive in all aspects of our lives. It leads to headaches, hypertension and stress, but now is the time to stop and tune out the noise, to press the mute button on life in order to reflect on who you are and where you're going.

The most joyful noise is silence. Being reflective means creating islands of silence to focus your mind. Your personal retreat can be measured in minutes, months or years. Silence is a way of coaxing us away from our constant doing. It removes the clutter from our lives to help us regain control. Silence drives us into ourselves to uncover those golden nuggets of who we are and how we really feel at our core.

Tara had had enough. She had to run away in order to catch up to herself. Two months later, she made the decision to take a break from her world. To abandon her life as she knew it. To escape to the north country for a couple of weeks on a river rafting experience—what organizers called an Alpha Excursion.

Her objective was to replenish her soul and review her life and, as well, to uncover those strategies that would add the meaning and clarity she was missing in her day-to-day life. She needed to get in touch with herself and her values. Her plan was to return with enduring principles that would become her touchstones, guiding her toward her goal of being fulfilled and contented.

Within three months, she found herself a lifetime away from the downtown jungle of Manhattan, at the Alpha Excursion outfitting camp preparing for her adventure. After a few days of intense instruction, she was given the bare essentials to survive her six-day journey. The most important tool she was given on the final day of her instructions would turn out to be a spiral notebook called an Alpha Log. Tara and her raft were then set adrift. She was alone on a river, streaming into an 'uncovery' of her own life.

Uncovery vs. Discovery

We are unique at birth. As we go through life, we tend to lose our uniqueness and become a statistic. We often hear of people 'discovering' themselves, where they've reached a pinnacle of self-knowledge. In reality, the process is not about discovering but *uncovering*. About peeling away the layers of what makes you *you*.

As each day goes by, we are very much influenced by the world around us—circumstances, people, our own self in various roles and capacities; in many ways we lead a life of other people's expectations. Over time we probably don't give sufficient thought to what that means, or what's happening to us. What we don't see are the pieces of ourselves that are buried and left behind as our strengths and talents are pushed to the back of our minds. In the extreme, we begin to morph ourselves and our identity into who we are not. When we lose the interior music expressing what makes us truly who we are, the disharmony manifests itself in stress, anxieties, tattered relationships and a dysfunctional life.

After her first day on the river, Tara was spent. Hour after hour, she drifted further and further away from the life she had known. The din and clutter of civilization began to fade and 'islands of silence' entered her brain. Thoughts began to flow in the form of questions, questions that led her to reflect deeply on her life. It was an hour before dusk when Tara made camp and took in some nourishment. A shower of sparks emitted from the firepit as she fed in another log. While evening settled in, she 'pulled up a rock' to recapture the thoughts that had washed through her on the broad avenue of the river.

She stripped the bark off a small branch, similar in size to the leg of an old wooden stool. With her survival knife, she instinctively carved the question *Where have I BEEN?*

If you don't have a focus or a goal for your own life, you'll be living by someone else's schedule. The less we are aware of ourselves—who we are and what we want—the more predisposed we are to allowing other persons or circumstances to determine what we're all about. It's referred to as "barnacle building." Over the years, we cover ourselves with multi-layers of barnacles. As barnacles begin to cover and weigh down a ship's hull, the vessel becomes less efficient, burns more energy and has less control over its direction. What started life as a sleek, fast and exciting ship, ends up as a tired, burdened barge, limping from port to port.

Life can cover each of us with enough barnacles that we lose sight of the real 'me' underneath. Sometimes it takes a traumatic experience to make us stop and take notice of ourselves, to realize how encumbered we are by life's barnacles. This is the time we would suggest you put yourself into dry dock, 'pull up a rock' and be reflective about where you've BEEN, where you're AT, and where you're GOING. It will be an enlightening experience as you begin to pull off the barnacles, when you can say, "Well, hello there. I knew you were down there somewhere but I had kind of lost touch with you."

The purpose of life is to *live life with purpose*. Clearing the barnacles from our lives is a good place to start, and we can start the process of clearing barnacles with the question "Where have I BEEN?"

The uncovery process begins with looking back to your earliest memories. In order for us to take control of where we're going, we have to look into our past to re-examine our footprints. *What are the defining moments, people and experiences that have shaped us?* We are the sum total of the choices we have made in life that have brought to us these moments, people and experiences.

A deep study of the question "Where have I BEEN?" may lead us to the realization that we sometimes adopt the persona of a character actor or an extra in life. Not being who we really know we are, can be the means through which we develop and accept a caricature of our true self. We end up in a mediocre life.

We'll illustrate the point with an example. An individual we'll call Ted grew up in a household where his father and grandfather were engineers. All through Ted's teenage years he felt the pressure of their expectations that he, too, would follow in their footsteps. In high school his teacher suggested to him that he would make a good engineer. His buddies all applied and graduated as engineers. So Ted listened to the 'markers' of his external world and concluded he should become an engineer, which he did. On graduation, Ted joined a technology firm. Over the years he began to feel a growing dissatisfaction with his life. On a beautiful mid-summer's night, sitting alone on the dock at his family's cottage, Ted took the first step toward being true to himself. "I hate engineering," he said aloud. " I've never enjoyed it and I don't want any of it now." This was the beginning of Ted's *uncovering* and his plan to change his career direction and raise the level of contentment with his life.

A Biography of Your Life

The first leg of your journey into managing your life with greater meaning and clarity is to uncover your past and become aware of those 'influencers' that have shaped who you are today. The clarifying process begins with writing your biography. Your story should address Tara's question: "Where have I BEEN?"

Chronicling your life could take a week, several weeks or a month. Buy yourself a notebook or large pad of paper, use napkins, envelopes, scraps of paper—anything you can get your hands on—to record your thoughts the moment they hit your brain. Always carry a writing utensil. If you're more comfortable with a computer, that's fine. The important thing is to get something written down, and what you want to be thinking about is not grammar, spelling or syntax. This is not about writing the world's greatest novel!

You don't start on a gloomy Sunday afternoon and say, "I'm going to write my biography." You may start your biography on a gloomy Sunday afternoon, but don't insist that you finish it that afternoon. Like any writing, there are moments when our hand doesn't move fast enough to record our thoughts. There are other times when thoughts feel as though they are weighted down with bags of lead, so you have to deal with that, but by the same token you have to set yourself a timetable for getting this done.

Start with your first memories of yourself. This is a fun exercise. Start today by writing the first things that passed through your head. When can I first remember me as *me*? Treat your first memories as your starting point; from there, write about the good times and the not-so-good times, because that's what life is all about.

In writing your own biography, it is important that you take your interests into consideration. What are the important components of your life? What are your special skills and talents? For the most part, our interests usually center on three areas of activity, namely: people, things and information.

An example of an activity centering on *people* would be coordinating the activity of others, be it in terms of our work or in terms of our family. The focus on *things* can be activities that draw our interest—for example, installing a computer system, painting or woodworking. Activities that involve *information* might include preparing for a presentation or engineering a power distribution system.

One of our clients summarized the experience of writing his biography this way:

> *Writing my biography cleaned up a lot of loose ends. All the pieces of my life presented themselves, which not only helped explain a lot of myself to me but showed how I had come to make the decisions I had made. Another interesting fact is that when I shared some of my life experiences and feelings with my family, what was important to me at the time wasn't important to them. In the end the biography clarified that 'this is how I am' and what drew me to do the things that I did.*

Your Values Determine the Person You've Become

When you are unsure of your own values, you are unsure of yourself. If you don't stand for something, you'll fall for anything. In addition to skills and interests, a critical question to ask while preparing your biography is "What are my values?"

Values are the mental standards we carry around in our heads; they assist us in making choices we believe are right for us in our everyday living. Values are guiding principles which give meaning to our lives. They cause us to investigate why certain things and activities are important to us. To value something is to assign a worth to it. Our values generate motivation, interest, desire and attitude. Values determine the person we've become…and the person we want to be.

Do I truly know what my values are? Can I cite experiences in my life where my values have played out? It is difficult to place ourselves in the right environments, or to change the environments in which we find ourselves, without a clear understanding of why we choose some conditions over others. In our breakneck world, with its growing uncertainties, staying the course means having a solid grounding in our core values.

Pieces of Your Future Are Preserved in Your Past

We are all created as individual souls. It's life that gives us a personality. Our personal history follows us and grows as we experience life. There is a point to our past. It knows everything about us.

Buried in your historical information is a treasury of data that becomes a directional guide in building your future. Knowing where you've been in life will help clarify the direction you should be heading for greater happiness and satisfaction. Like Tara, it's time to pull your raft into shore. 'Pull up a rock' and spend silent time reflecting on the story of your past. This information is critical in developing your plans for the future.

Writing your biography gives you the opportunity to review how your life has changed over the years. Through the magic of your own storytelling, you'll find your history interesting and unique, full of wisdom in color and dimension. You will punctuate how you have grown through your experiences, how resilient you are and how much you've learned. Trust the process: Life is always more than what it seems; you are more than what you've become.

Thoughtwork Exercises

Destination: Writing your biography

Bio Lifeline – Where have you BEEN? This exercise will help you to begin the process of writing your own history. Begin by drawing a timeline (as illlustrated on page 34). Divide the line by the number of years in your life. The bottom of the line represents your earliest memory.

To the left of the line, note the defining moments in your life —the people, experiences, choices (good and bad, i.e. education and career choices), skills and talents that have influenced and shaped the person you are today. These are your **External Life Influencers**.

To the right of the line, add your **Internal Life Influencers** which are:

 Emotional Reading—To each of the defining moments that appear on the left of the Bio Lifeline, write a description of how you felt about what had occurred at and between those experiences. Describe how comfortable or uncomfortable you felt around each defining moment.

Also add a *Values Epilogue* statement. Go back over your lifeline and add a layer over everything that we'll call a Values Epilogue— a description of how your values were tested, impacted, defined or changed around each defining moment. Describe how each circumstance confronted your values system. For example, during your childhood, what were the major forces/factors shaping your beliefs and values? In your self-image mirror, what do you see as your five most dominant values? What values were tested or impacted at this stage of your life? Did this influence a change in your values system, serve to confirm your values, or force you to adopt new values?

As you begin to empty yourself of your experiences, concentrate on how each notation has had an impact on your life. You'll find that you add additional 'defining life moments' and influencers as your memories begin to unfreeze.

Where you are AT today

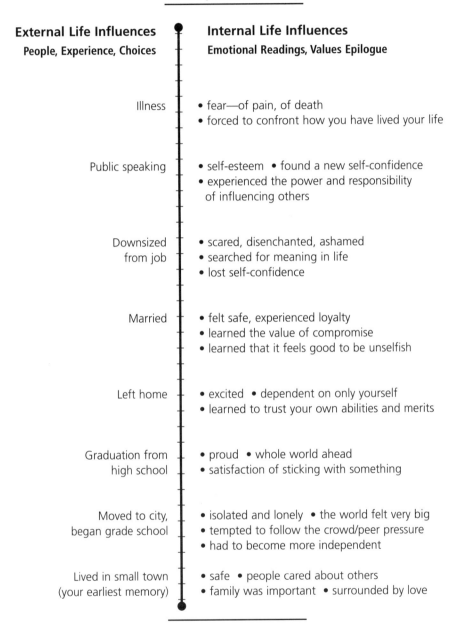

External Life Influences
People, Experience, Choices

Internal Life Influences
Emotional Readings, Values Epilogue

Illness
- fear—of pain, of death
- forced to confront how you have lived your life

Public speaking
- self-esteem • found a new self-confidence
- experienced the power and responsibility of influencing others

Downsized from job
- scared, disenchanted, ashamed
- searched for meaning in life
- lost self-confidence

Married
- felt safe, experienced loyalty
- learned the value of compromise
- learned that it feels good to be unselfish

Left home
- excited • dependent on only yourself
- learned to trust your own abilities and merits

Graduation from high school
- proud • whole world ahead
- satisfaction of sticking with something

Moved to city, began grade school
- isolated and lonely • the world felt very big
- tempted to follow the crowd/peer pressure
- had to become more independent

Lived in small town (your earliest memory)
- safe • people cared about others
- family was important • surrounded by love

Bio LifeLine

A.

The Second Leg

Where Am I AT?

It's only when we realize that life is taking us nowhere that it begins to have meaning.

— P.D. Ouspensky

Tara's first night did not go well. Her sleep had been restless. Every flap of the tent in the night wind or scratch of a branch playing against the nylon walls drove her deeper into her sleeping bag. Her axe and flashlight were constant companions. Tara poked her head out of the tent to face the dawn of her second day. She breathed deeply, filling her lungs with the moist northern air.

The tent perspired with the heavy dew that had descended on the woodland overnight. Morning fog shrouded her camp. She was barely able to discern the ancient forest bordering her firepit. Stripped of her corporate blanket, she withdrew to the tent, feeling alone, with the world closing in around her. She gathered her thoughts and swallowed the slight taste of fear that enveloped her. "It's all right," she counseled herself. "It's my choice to be here." The voices of fear within her were silenced.

As the morning brightened, the veil of fog lifted gently, coloring the world around her. She eyed a parade of small footprints that had explored her campsite during the night. Calling cards from foxes or raccoons littered the site. The notion of wild animals roaming within inches of her sleeping body filled her with muted excitement. She congratulated herself for stashing her foodstuffs off the ground as she had been instructed in orientation training. After a cold breakfast, she packed up her tent and loaded the raft for the second leg of her journey.

Before boarding, Tara hesitated, savoring the moment. It was then she noticed the deafening silence of the natural world. Her body was so addicted to a life saturated with background noise that this environment felt unnatural and eerie. She had gone cold turkey from a high-decibel life to where she had to strain to hear the sounds around her.

It wasn't a sound that caught her attention but a sudden tugging of the rope in her hand as the river's current grabbed at the raft, pulling and teasing it away from her. She jumped in, leaving her first night behind.

If we think more than superficially about it, human beings are essentially acculturated to fear. If that's the case, it's no wonder we don't want to stop those telephone poles from flashing by. We don't want to face up, in any serious way, to what fills our lives. "Should I be doing what I'm doing, namely running along at this fast pace, having to do more and more in every way, in both my life at work and at home?" People who take the time to listen to themselves base their choices on what they care about. They feel good about their decisions. "Whose life is it anyway? Am I living my life or am I living the life of a whole host of other people who are directly or indirectly a part of my world?"

Around midmorning, Tara pulled into shore to journal her thoughts in her Alpha Log. "Life is a river," she wrote. "We are ruled by the ebb and flow of our emotional tides driven by Internet time. We get caught in the rushing current, unable to escape the rapid flow. We go where the river takes us, barely negotiating the rocks and rapids that can do us in."

And so, Tara filled her day, and the pages of her Alpha Log, pondering her past and documenting those defining moments in her life—the people, choices and achievements that had influenced the fabric of her character. Nature had lured her into an inner silence. In order to hear her true nature, she knew she had to be still. She thought about those experiences that enthused her with freedom and joy. She was determined to reclaim those feelings.

Tara also understood that knowing where we come from is indispensable to reconnect with whom we are inside. We need to understand and acknowledge this information before we can move forward with confidence, focus and determination. The process not only involves uncovering and understanding who we are but also accepting who we've become. That necessitates travel through our past to where we've been. Taking the first steps to write her Alpha Log biography helped Tara come to terms with important life experiences and gave her the opportunity to listen to her inner voice. She walked the paths of her history, recording what life was like along the way and the circumstances that brought her to where she was at this milestone in her life. As she wrote, she could feel herself rising above the landscape of her life to a vantage point where she could reflect on the totality of who she was. She sensed the deeper meaning to the choices she had made that led her to the present. It felt like flying at 35,000 feet.

Her last journal entry of the day was recorded while nursing a mug of hot chocolate by firelight. Tara was exhausted but exhilarated. She 'pulled up a rock' and sought out the branch whittled the night before. Her hand ran across the question she had carved, *Where have I BEEN*? "I've been losing myself," she murmured. Tara procured another tree branch similar in size and carved into her second leg of wood the question *Where am I AT?*

We all go through life in our own way. Every one of us has an imperceptible momentum to our lives, filled with rhythm and harmony. Everything we've done, felt and accomplished in life shapes who we are. If we reflect on who we are, we'll realize we have given our life meaning. Collecting and accumulating our "bin of data" from our past is a clarifying process. But we haven't necessarily given our life a purpose. What would be the purpose of your life from the viewpoint of where you're AT today?

The question forces us to look at who we are in a most reflective way. The lesson we find is that it's hard to look at ourselves objectively and with confidence if we've never done it before. Exactly how much vision can we have for ourselves if our nose is always to the spinning grindstone of this world?

The simple, powerful fact is that understanding your past helps give you a fix on future direction. Thinking about your positive attributes and dreams begins to scratch the surface of who you are, what you have to offer the world, and where you want to be in future. That's why the past is important to your future. Visualize, if you will, walking across the North Pole where all you see up ahead are miles and miles of untrodden, barren snowscape. If you were to look over your shoulder, you would see the wandering path of your footsteps indicating the direction from which you've come. The Inuit people who live on Canada's most northern shores erect lifelike figures of rock called Inukshuk (pronounced IN-OOK-SHOOK). It's an Inuit word meaning 'the image of man.' One of the Inukshuk's purposes is to serve as a directional marker on treeless horizons to guide those who follow. Likewise, your footprints are the impressions of your past that serve now to give you a bearing. They help you find your direction so that you're not running in circles; they also tell you how far you've come. Along the way have been personal Inukshuks or markers where you've learned, struggled, grown, succeeded and experienced joy and pain.

We further define to ourselves who we are as we travel the road of life. Each forward step we take leaves an imprint filled with experience and insight where we can glean new wisdom and understanding as we dare to release our yesterdays and step into our future days.

There is an increased craving among people today for balance in their lives—a greater dimension in their day that encompasses career, family and community. They want to find meaning outside their workplace through involvement in the larger world. We refer to it as leading a 360-degree life, one that's multi-dimensional.

The 'you mentality' is the means to lift your head above your desk or away from your computer screen for a higher perspective of who you are and what you can accomplish. Your increased peripheral vision helps you "see" the opportunities around you not yet realized. Raise your antennae and add a set of new lenses to view the world from higher ground.

Our Traditional Touchstones Power Our Lives

When looking inside ourselves and reflecting on our personal and family history, we can pick out touchstones from our heritage and upbringing that define who we are. These touchstones represent our values and traditions, and remind us of "defining moments" and people in our lives in terms of who we've become. For example, personal touchstones could include an athletic award, a school ring, the family photo album, a favorite uncle, a close friend or a mentor.

Touchstones give us confidence and a sense of belonging; they remind us of our accomplishments. As learning events that help shape our lives, they can also be positive or negative. One individual who grew up on a farm feels the need to return to an important touchstone of his—the family homestead. Every so often, when life gets too hectic, he goes back to sit on the tractor and stroll the fields. In a life filled with uncertainty, going back provides the breathing space to reassess the value of his life in the comfort of a familiar, secure and controlled setting. It re-anchors him to those events in his life that more closely define him.

Our past is constantly expanding. Every once in a while, it's important to reach back and reconnect with our touchstones.

Tara treasured the memory of summers growing up at the family cottage. Her high-powered career meant she had little time for the cottage as part of her adult life. Shortly before the cottage was sold, she visited one last time. She stood alone on the old porch facing the boathouse. Her mind took her back over thirty years to when she was 12 years old and helping her dad complete a small rowboat that bore her name.

Tara loved the aroma of the old boathouse. To this day, the smell of fresh-cut cedar always takes her back inside that boathouse. She was her father's 'first mate,' helping him bring life to his design. She can hear the whoosh of her wood plane as it skinned the strips of planking; she can feel the delicate touch of the wood shavings curling at her feet.

That summer, *Tara* was launched. The rowboat's maiden voyage coincided with Tara's father's quest to have his 12-year-old daughter attempt to swim to an island in the middle of the lake. Halfway to her island destination, Tara paused to rest and felt the cold water circling her feet. She looked back at the prow of the rowboat shadowing her. Every breath brought an ache to her lungs. The dock of the family cottage was now only a speck in the distance. The island was shimmering on the horizon, teasing her on. "Daddy, it's too far, I can't make it, it's too far." Her father rested the oars, his face leaning over the side.

"OK, we'll just rest for a minute. You can do it, Tara, I know you can. Why, look at how much farther you've come since your last attempt." He studied his young daughter. "I'll tell you what, we won't go to the island today." With that, her father took a stub of an old branch lying in the bottom of the boat and tossed it out so it splashed a small distance in front of Tara. "There now, just swim to the branch, that's all."

Tara strengthened her will and swam to the branch. She passed it over to her father. "Tara, that was very good. Let's try it one more time."

Tara struggled to keep her mouth above water. "But Daddy, I'm really tired."

"I know, honey, I won't throw it as far this time." Tara heard the splash and struggled to the floating branch, totally exhausted. Her father told her how wonderful she was and wrapped her in a towel as they headed back to the cottage. She never made it to the island that day. Even though she had swam further than she ever had before, there was always a lingering feeling of having disappointed her father.

But on this day, years later, she reminded herself of the value of challenging who she was—that going beyond what she thought was possible was now a part of who she was. Standing on the porch, remembering what had been, Tara looked again at the island. She walked to the end of the dock, stripped off her clothes and finished the swim.

I'm the Only Me Who Will Ever Be

Emblazoned on a T-shirt are the words: I am the only me who will ever be. We are each a unique blend of talents, skills and potential. So questions such as "Who am I?" and "How should I use my life?" take on enormous significance when you look at yourself as the only 'you' who will ever be on this planet.

We use past information as a guide—not as an unquestioned authority—to future travels. If we take our past experience too literally, we'll only continue the way we are. The effort is to use the past to catch up to ourselves, and then move forward to the present time, to address the question of "Where am I AT?"

When we stop to think about where we're AT in the world today, in many cases we say, "Where I'm AT is rather confusing, because it's *not* where I'm AT. What I mean is that it's not where I want to be." Well, where do you want to be? In the long-running television series *Cheers*, the character Norm was asked that question. He responded with, "It's a dog-eat-dog world and I'm wearing Milkbone underwear." If that's your circumstance, it's time to 'pull up a rock' and mull over the question, "If this is where I'm AT, how comfortable am I with my AT position?"

Let's say you measured where you're AT in your world of work—satisfaction, challenge and reward—on a scale of 1 to 10, with 10 being high. You rate yourself a 4. Would that suggest you should spend some time ratcheting up that marker to a 7 or 8? Or, are you OK with your marker being at 4?" People at that level on the scale are at least comfortable with boredom because that's where they're at in their life: bored. They put themselves on automatic pilot and accept life at that level. They remain at that level out of fear or anxiety connected to change. They perceive that the pain of staying where they are isn't as great as the pain they would endure if they decided to change—so they stay put and accept the life they've got.

Life at a 4 lacks spontaneity, a certain amount of joy, a certain amount of happiness, a certain amount of fun. And that fun word is an interesting one. In today's world we often hear the statement "This isn't fun anymore," and it frequently applies to our feelings about our work environment.

Author Tom Brown Jr. noted, "People who stay on the same paths in life will eventually wear themselves into ruts...a complacency to life born of false security, comfort and monotony of that path. Soon the ruts become so deep that we can no longer see over the sides. They see neither danger nor beauty, only the path before them, nor do they abandon that path so often traveled for fear of losing their security and entering the land of the unknown." The deep, inner self is at the apex of your reality. The difficulty for most people lies in setting aside the 'outside' self that is culturally conditioned with belief and behavior values acquired and imposed over the years, in order to find their inner self, free of all these restrictions.

The World Changes Without Our Permission

The AT position can be our most uncomfortable stance. It sits between "Where have I BEEN?"—the Past—and "Where am I GOING?"—the Future. It represents the undulating present, filled with drama and interruptions. It's uncomfortable because we are living the moment, right now, and the moment is shaking under our feet and forever changing and asking us for directions. In many cases it is changing without our permission and without our agreement, changing for the sake of changing. When we look at the past, well, that's settled, that's there. But the AT position is very much in our face, and most of us would say, "The here and now keeps moving. I can't even reach out and grab it and make it stop. I have no control."

There's a wonderful adage: "Life happens while we're making other plans." Coming to grips with meaning in our reactive lives creates a sense of trying to hang onto a handful of Jell-O. It just keeps slipping and squeezing between our fingers. That is how our AT position can feel. However, if we've 'pulled up a rock" and spent some time reflecting on where we've BEEN, taking a look at our AT position will be somewhat more stabilizing and less frightening.

Peter Urs Bender, in his book *GUTFEELING*, noted what T.S. Eliot called "the still point of the turning world." He meant that when you are properly 'centered' in yourself, YOU are the point around which the world turns. The real universe starts from within.

Where Am I AT Now?

Where you're AT boils down to the relationship you have with yourself and how that meshes with the life you're presently living. The Bio Lifeline in the previous chapter's Thoughtwork Exercises will have amplified your life and brought you to a higher level of consciousness regarding the unique attributes of your 'inner being.' The following Thoughtwork Exercises will help discern how far outside yourself you're living—in your AT position.

Thoughtwork Exercises

Destination: To clarify where you're AT

Draw Your Self-Portrait

We each live life one frame at a time. Sometimes we are in the foreground, sometimes in the background, and sometimes we are even out of focus. This exercise will stand you in front of a virtual camera for a self-portrait that puts your uniqueness in context with 'where am I AT' in living life today.

On a blank piece of paper, draw a 'stick' figure in the centre of the page (this represents you). Write this heading above your figure: Self-Portrait of the Unique Me.

On the left of the figure, list a snapshot of your values, talents, insights and characteristics from your Bio Lifeline. The list will include a compilation of the words that describe your inner self—the person underneath all those barnacles.

On the right of the figure, using the information on the left as a reference, list those things in your life today that are:

a)   in disharmony with the desires and character of the real you; and

b)   those things you are tolerating which are contradictory to who you really are.

Self-Portrait of Unique Me

Reference the previous
"Where Have I BEEN" lifeline
(see pages 32 to 34)

Snapshot of my values, talents,
strengths and characteristics

Disharmonies in my life
that aren't the real me

Things I am tolerating
which are contradictory
to who I really am

What is all this telling me?

Question the Work in Your Life

In addition to completing your self-portrait, contemplate these "where am I AT" questions for your Alpha Log. Find an 'island of silence,' away from the hustle and bustle of daily living. Force yourself to listen to your inner self as you grope to answer the questions. Be honest. The feelings and notations in your journal should be of high integrity. In other words, be truthful as you search for the answer to these tough questions. It is a beginning strategy to have your life and livelihood flow from the same source.

1. Do I experience joy in my work...under what circumstances, how often, how can this be increased?

2. When did I first feel drawn to the kind of work I'm doing? Has that feeling increased or decreased over the years? Have I lost touch with my feelings? Am I a slave to my work?

3. Is my work merely a job or is it a vocation, calling or role? How do I know the answer to this question?

4. How am I emptied at work? How does 'nothingness' happen? What is my response to nothingness at work?

5. How does my environment affect my work?

6. What do I learn at work? Is it a learning experience for me? In what ways is it a learning experience for others?

7. If I were to leave my work today, what difference would it make to my spiritual growth?

8. What are my drifts of instinct and natural attractions?

9. What is my greatest inner need?

These are not easy questions to answer, but don't be put off by them. At least *ask* yourself these questions; the answers will come in time. As each day begins, remember to take your life lessons with you. The keys to knowing and achieving the goals you want for your future are wrapped up in the wisdom of knowing where you've BEEN and where you're AT. Only through this deep self-awareness can you answer the next question: Where am I GOING?

G.

The Third Leg

Where Am I GOING?

There is no tougher challenge that we face than to accept personal responsibility for not only what we are but also what we can be.

— David McNally

As Tara's day advanced, the clouds melted and a magnificent sun warmed her unprotected head. Leaning back on the canvas shoulders of her raft, she soaked up the warmth, relinquishing control to the meandering river. She became a passenger viewing the landscape flowing by. A light-footed fox trotted along the water's edge. Otters blissfully looped in and out of the water. The occasional slap of a beaver's tail signaled her approach, and the black specks of unknown noses sank out of sight.

A gigantic cow moose and her calf shattered the surface as water lily delicacies were yanked from their roots, scattering a flock of resting waterfowl. A magnificent osprey soared high into the sky until it almost disappeared from sight, and then suddenly dove straight into the water, emerging seconds later with a fish in its talons. Tara was enraptured by the spirit of the place. At one point, the stately forest gave way to a wild meadow resplendent with fireweed that had healed the land after a devastating burn.

But rivers have their moods. The raft began to pick up speed. Tara righted herself, tightening her hands around the paddle. The shoreline began to grow giant boulders just below the waterline, and bulwarks of rocky cliffs took form, cutting the river in half. She had a decision to make. To her right, the river was drawn into a healthy stream that disappeared quietly into the ancient forest. To her left were the growl of rapids and cascades of powerful, foaming white water. Sharp edges of rock knifed the river, and twisted outcroppings of trees hung precariously from the towering cliffs. Tara stabbed at the water with her paddle, trying desperately to direct her raft into the headwaters of the stream. But her craft was unable to resist the raging waters. She was helpless against the pull of the current's tow. All she could do now was hang on as she ran the gauntlet and sudden fury of the boiling rapids. She held her breath. "Oh God, where am I going?"

When we stop to take inventory, the reality is that we live a life soaked in a torrent of noise. Big noise that comes disguised as information. Is it any wonder we can't think straight? The truth is that 90 percent of that 'information' is strictly clutter and virtually useless to creating the future we want for ourselves. If we believe all we hear, we run the risk that we may attach ourselves to meaningless things. Like Tara, we are caught up in the swift current of life and swept along with very little control over where we're going or what shape we'll be in when we get there. We end up in spirit-crushing work that may provide financial success, but leaves us unsatisfied.

Your history is a compass, not a map. When looking to the future, you reflect on and draw from your past experience. Interpreting your information from the first two legs, you should begin to feel a sense of future direction. How you see yourself today is critically important to who you'll become. The key is to pay attention to your growing bin of data and respect its authority. Just like any other trip you take, you must first envision the destination before you begin the journey. It's no different in life or career planning. You use the information, images and ideas from your life's experience as internal drivers to propel you in the direction you want to go. As you continue to develop your quiver of skills, your arrows will fly closer to the center of the goal you have set for yourself.

Using a biblical context for planning your future, consider Noah and his ark. Remember that when Noah built the ark it wasn't raining; here was somebody who wasn't caught up in the fast lane. He obviously did a little thinking: *If there's going to be this great rush of water, maybe I'd better think about some survival tactics.* You could say that Noah took his own self-imposed sabbatical, thought about life in the broader sense, pulled up a rock and seriously considered the question Where am I GOING?

Our B.A.G. of Life

Grey Owl's best-selling book, *The Men of the Last Frontier*, described his journeys into the wilderness this way:

> *Travelling in an unpeopled wilderness calls for an intense concentration on the trail behind, a due regard for the country ahead and a memory that recalls every turn made, and that can recognize a ridge, gully or stream crossed previously and at another place. Swinging off the route to avoid swamps and other deviations must be accomplished without losing sight of the one general direction, meanwhile the trail unrolls behind like a ball of yarn, one end of which is camp, the other in your hands.*

We have to take time to reflect if we are ever to really get to know ourselves. Our learning about ourselves blossoms in the middle of silent reflections. Distilling the wisdom from 'B' (where we've BEEN) and 'A' (where we're AT) brings clarity to the vision of 'G' (where we're GOING). The wisdom of Grey Owl calls for intense concentration on the trail behind: where have you been, what is your history? The future is undiscovered; where you set up camp is in your hands. Recording your history helps you recognize and avoid those obstacles that hinder your progress, to intimately know your strengths and those things that fill you with joy. In essence, we've been working on our B.A.G. of life.

The wild river at last calmed down in the fading light of day. Tara had survived the violent water, but her body was played out. She pulled her drenched equipment onto shore, pitched her tent beneath an overhang of rock and lit a fire to dry out.

The day was the most physically challenging she had ever encountered. This tiredness was a good tiredness, though, not like the mental fatigue she suffered at the office. It hit home that the change of environment had changed her perception of her life. She suddenly realized how manipulated she was by the extreme demands of her job and the lack of control she had over her existence. Every morning she stepped into the game of life and became a pawn. Strangely similar, she thought, to the whitewater world that had just challenged her, putting her in peril at every moment.

But this place spoke to her differently and demanded different things from her in order to survive. The perpetual buzzing and cacophony of Manhattan was gone. She had escaped the urban pressures, transported by a river that was speaking to the soul of its traveler. The noise enveloping her now was almost soundless—without harsh, sharp edges; it was smooth, round and soulful. The wind softly stirred the treetops. The resting water massaged the pebbles on shore. It was a symphony of nature whose harmony touched her at a profound level. Her body may have been spent, but her mind was alive with clarity. "My life is not really real," she reasoned, "When I die it all disappears." Tara struggled with the thought, "What is real is the legacy I leave behind. What do I want my family and friends to think of me after I'm gone?"

From her backpack, Tara removed the one luxury item she had brought with her on the excursion. It was a non-judgmental friend, her portable CD player. Depressing the 'play' button released the sound of her favorite jazz music; it wafted softly through the darkening forest. She searched for a perfect branch and performed her evening ritual. Unsheathing her survival knife, she carved the question *Where am I GOING?*

Interpreting Your Bin of Data

The GOING question is a more difficult one when compared to thinking about where we have BEEN and where we are AT. It can be less difficult if we've made a concerted effort with the uncovering process so as to create a bin of data on the 'real me.' We can certainly begin to interpret some of this data we have about ourselves and use that to creatively craft our future, bearing in mind that we don't have absolute control. But we have far more control than we ever realize, and that is a liberating certitude!

We draw on this bin of data to scope out a future that makes sense based on the exploration and the uncovering we have already done, and begin again to connect the dots. Out of this should come two, three or four clear options appropriate to pursue. Some will be more viable than others, but at least we will have pinpointed those destinations appropriate for ourselves. Out of those, we develop some real-life action plans to validate particular future directions and options.

Cam Cole, a columnist for the *National Post*, reported that Mike Weir, Canada's rapidly reborn 32-year-old PGA Tour star, wanted to turn his game from ordinary in October to fabulous by February. To do that, Mike Weir took a self-imposed break to help him refocus. Mike sat around thinking for three months. "It didn't change by accident," Mike stated, "it was a committed decision to have a better attitude and enjoy the game more." That's it, no psychologist, no visits to his swing coach.

"I think when you try to be too perfect in this game you put too much pressure on yourself," he said, "and I think that's what I fell into last year. Just trying too hard is basically what it boiled down to. And this year I just said, let's go out and

enjoy the game and just see what happens, not try to do anything outside of my capabilities really."

Following that, Weir shot 66 to beat his opponent (Howell) in
a sudden-death playoff to win the Nissan Open.

Refresh the Pond

Mike Weir began by removing himself from the clutter and
noise of today's world. He left to inhabit a three-month 'island
of silence' to reflect on and refresh the pond of information
about himself and how he got to be where he was. By reaching
into your own bin of data, you will uncover the story around
your uniqueness and use this information to explore options to
increase the level of future performance and contentment.

The act of scripting your story gets you into your spirit. Ask
yourself probing questions such as, "What do I really want to
do in my life? Does it seem hard to tell sometimes?" One way
of helping envision the inklings of your true inner self is to
clear away all the turbulence, to refresh yourself and just do
some old-fashioned 'blue sky' forecasting. The answers are
there inside you—they just need a path through all the clutter
so they can reach the surface.

In your own Alpha Log, jot down your answer to this question: What would you start doing tomorrow if you KNEW there was absolutely NO CHANCE OF FAILING?

At her peaceful campsite, Tara sat back and pondered the dutiful roles she had played in her life. She was a daughter, a go-getter, a friend, an achiever, a caregiver. Who am I supposed to be, she thought? When can I know and claim the person I really am—and want to be? The process of journaling in her Alpha Log had her eavesdropping on her inner soul, to listen to what it was telling her. It began to steer her back on course.

Reflections on Your Inner Beings

You are more than who you are at work. In terms of addressing the question of where you are going in life, every person is a unique package of experience and potential. Each of us behaves in a wonderfully complex and multi-faceted way. Just as a diamond's radiance reflects in such dazzling and different ways off the various surfaces of the stone, people also reflect their inner brilliance in rich and subtle ways against the different roles they assume each day. We are, in fact, comprised of a number of inner beings, which we will call Multiple Me's.

We believe your mind is already organized to support your role at the moment, whether it be as a parent or child, friend or foe, boss or subordinate, volunteer or paid help. The wisdom of 'G' in this leg of the journey asks you also to think about and define your Multiple Me's.

The Multiple Me exercise that follows asks you to think about what other roles and dreams you seek for yourself. Each of your individual "me's" needs to be nourished with time, effort and management. Your decisions and choices in daily living will determine the amount of time/effort/management you put towards each of your Multiple Me's.

Like a living tree, each year you add a ring of growth. Over time, how you allocate your time and energy ultimately shapes who you are.

New growth takes time. It is not subject to a formula. The calendar of time, energy and management needed to create significant changes in a Multiple Me segment is different for every person. Some changes happen overnight, others over months or years. The growing point in natural plants happens annually with the change of seasons as the buds begin to form and blossom. The growing point in humans is also stimulated by an environment of change but is not run by a biological clock. By our nature, human beings are more reluctant than plants to embrace change on a pre-determined schedule. But, if you don't have the courage, will or desire to make or deal with change, you are forced to retreat to the fleeting comfort of an ultimately unsatisfying AT position.

In moments of reflection, we find that few of our early dreams extend very far into our mature years, and when they run out, our expectancy usually shrinks and shrivels. *Most of us run out of script long before we die.* Psychologist Carl Jung tells us that "We can't live the afternoon of life according to the program of life's morning; for what was great in the morning will be little at evening, and what in the morning was true will at evening have become a lie."

The important fact is that we still have a choice, both as communities of people and at the very personal level of life planning. Our personal choice in how we see the world has immense implications for our home life, success at work, and effectiveness as a human being. It is important we understand and accept the challenge of how we can get the flow of change into our life and find new promises, horizons, resources and passions throughout all our years.

Wise words from C.F. Kettering may be enlightening: "I expect to spend the rest of my life in the future so I want to be reasonably sure what kind of future it's going to be. That is my reason for planning." Remember, within the boundaries of change that are enveloping your life today are opportunities to strengthen your character and your potential to bloom. Embrace change…it never ends.

Thoughtwork Exercises

Destination: To explore the possibilities of where you're GOING in the different segments of your life

1. Illustrate your pool of Multiple Me's.

Begin by drawing a circle on a page. Divide the circle into four segments. Write within each segment one of your Multiple Me's. For example, one segment could be defined as Career Me, another Family Me, Spiritual Me or Adventure Me.

You can divide your pool into as many segments as necessary to represent all the Multiple Me's of your life.

2. Your next step is to look at each Multiple Me.

This is an important step. Be sure to give yourself good, quiet reflective time to consider the **growth action steps** below:

a) ***State the vision*** you want to achieve for yourself in each of your Multiple Me segments. Your Vision Statement records the specific desire to which you will commit time, energy, dollars and focus toward enriching each segment. For example, the Vision statement for your Adventure Me segment may be stated as: to raft North America's five best whitewater rivers over the next five years. The most important thinking skills at this point are imagination, thinking 'large' and being positive and enthusiastic.

b) ***Define inner values*** that support that vision. This is where you list the inner drives for your behavior in each segment. Using the Adventure Me example, these inner values could include love of the outdoors, maintenance of a balanced life, caring for body and soul, a keen interest in environmental issues...

c) **_Characterize your reality_** of present-day life in each segment. This involves looking at your vision statements for each Multiple Me. Write a description of how you feel about where things are headed. Are you getting closer to the vision you want for yourself or drifting further away from it?

d) **_List the obstacles and opportunities_** associated with the time, energy and management required to achieve your vision.

Time:
What are the factors relating to clock and calendar?

Energy:
What factors affect your mental and physical energy, stamina and spirit, to keep you active and enthusiastic?

Management:
What are the given circumstances you must uncover and consider in order to take focused action and allocate time and energy to make your vision happen?

e) **_Plan change actions and options for the future._**
Happiness for a raindrop might be to die in a river. What would make you happy? This step is where you

plan your new definition of success. List specific
activities you must complete, including the order and
time you must complete them in, to successfully
achieve your vision for this segment.

3.   Dialogue with others.

Once you've developed your change action plans/options,
share your story with others. Use them as a sounding
board for your thoughts. Their feedback will be valuable
in throwing some light and perspective on your options,
and will ultimately build a reinforcing foundation of confidence in your choices.

*...listen to the people who love you. Your company
does not love you. Your friends and your family
love you. Ask them, 'How do you think I'm doing?
How do you see me right now?' They will paint the
picture of truth about you.*

> — a quote from an article in *Fast Company* magazine
> attributed to Mary Lou Quinlan, ex-CEO of a
> major advertising agency.

The Remaining Three Legs:
Getting Your A.C.T. Together

Life is full of change. The good passes, but so does the bad. Nothing remains the same in this unstable world. When we are down at the bottom of the pit of despair, the only way to go is up. If we only wait a little, the cycle—the endless, unfailing tide of things—will sweep us up again. Without darkness we would not appreciate the light when it comes.

— Kristin Zambucka

Tara awakened to a peaceful morning and emerged from her down-filled cocoon. She poked her head outside the tent where she was confronted with the musty odor of damp wood and the smell of the spicy pine pitch. The silence of morning was all-embracing. There was no shrill of her alarm, no phone calls, no blaring radio, no office politics, no one to notice her absence. This was a place of intimacy, a private wilderness where one's own presence was always felt. She thought about the connections and relationships that nature extends to all living things, much like a huge circle.

She pulled out her Alpha Log and noted her thoughts about the contrast of how the world of work connects to life and how what she was experiencing now was different:

> *Work is a connection of artificial, man-made, technical points. In contrast, everything here has a natural connection. The woodland is companion to the river…the river nourishes the ocean…the ocean breathes clouds into the sky…and the sky envelops all living things. The environment here thrives on the quality of symbiotic co-existence. Can work be the same…?*

After her morning meal, Tara packed up. The silky mist portrayed the river as a strange, surreal highway that beckoned her onward. She paddled to the heart of the running current, letting it play her along. She refined her tactics, piloting her raft in and out of the current, feeling more confident in controlling her direction.

"The learning is in the doing," she repeated to herself, remembering something she had read. "More learning comes out of an experience than goes into it. Next time, I'll *choose* to chance the rapids!"

Around midmorning, the river lost some of its vigor, allowing her to relax and thumb through her Alpha Log. She reread her notes describing the memory of the twists and bends of her life—where she had BEEN, where she was AT and where she was GOING. Tara had come to relish her thoughtful silence and the notions that swam inside her mind.

The river zigzagged past an unfolding landscape heavy with pine, aspen and birch. Pristine water, studded with imposing gray boulders and fringes of lush grassy marshlands, mirrored the color of forest and sky. A wisp of fur drew Tara's attention to the shore. Her eyes penetrated the dark gloom of the woods. Floating on an invisible forest trail was a huge timber wolf, its ghostlike movement keeping pace with the speed of her raft. Prior to her Alpha Excursion, Tara had surfed the Internet for information on aspects of living in the wild. She remembered the information on *Canis Lupus*—the wolf. The more she had studied wolves, the more she admired these remarkable creatures.

She recalled that the social structure of a wolf pack was extremely sophisticated. "A wolf pack's social structure could serve as a business model," she thought. The first rule of the pack is that it's made up of leaders and followers. The pack's 'top management' is referred to as the Alpha pair—a male and female. The Alphas dominate the pack; all the followers are subordinate to them. "But the pack behaves as a 'super organism,' cooperatively making it possible for more animals to survive. In most human work environments, we see a kind of 'predatory leadership'—it's every man for himself."

The animal was captivating. "It must be an Alpha," she exclaimed aloud. Tara recalled that any wolf could become an Alpha, but for it to happen, the wolf must leave its original pack, and stake out an unoccupied territory.

Tara wondered, "Is this wolf on an Alpha Excursion of its own—like me?" The lone wolf continued its shadowy journey through the trees. Tara opened her Alpha Log and recorded her thoughts:

Alpha is all about leadership...taking back control, finding our own territory and becoming our own leader.
I must become and remain the dominant Alpha in my life.

Authors Gary and Joanie McGuffin, in their book *Journey Into the Ancient Forest*, state: *Living for awhile at the speed of nature, as we do on a long journey, makes us more aware of the world around us. When we smell, taste, touch, hear and feel the world as intimately as children, our role becomes more than that of onlooker. Our sense of realities of all living creatures is both astounding and humbling. We must use our ability to imagine ourselves under the skin of a cougar, or in the seed of a pine, or in a drop of water travelling from ocean to sky and through the bodies of all living matter because we are all of these things all of the time.*

The Sound of Her Heart Beating

While she was climbing the corporate ladder, Tara gave little thought to the truly important things in life; she thought only of money and power. But now, she began to hear her soul speak to her: Inside the nucleus of power resides vulnerability. She had learned that you were only as good as your last report to shareholders, your last customer interaction, your last sale or project.

It afforded Tara security knowing she had a big job in a big office. It was what she knew. It was also a life she thought she couldn't live without. By stepping out of the Manhattan jungle during her sabbatical, her reflections clarified she could live without it. Tara realized she had actually chosen the fate that she had previously thought had chosen her. Now she needed to make different choices if her future was going to change.

As Tara reread her Alpha Log, it altered her inner environment. She decided to take a different view of her notes, reviewing them not as author and participant, but as an observer. It was a way to disconnect briefly by crawling inside her own skin to uncover and authenticate what it all meant to her. What could she glean from the past that would clarify her true nature and connect her to more joy and happiness in the future? Had her definition of success changed or would she just climb back up into the Manhattan CEO machine?

Tara stripped the bark from three new branches that had now become part of her survival gear. She began examining her bin of data, searching for answers that would transition her life over the next horizon. On each she carved one of three probing questions:

What have I really ACCOMPLISHED?
How did I CREATE what I did?
What were my inner TRIUMPHS?

Repeating Tara's three new questions to yourself will force you to step back and become very much in touch with your B.A.G. of data. The initial three legs we've talked about develop the bin of data on your history—where you've BEEN, where you're AT, and where you're GOING in terms of the choices you think appropriate to pursue.

The last three legs tighten up your A.C.T. to prepare you for the future in giving credence to the things you've accomplished, how you accomplished them and how you grew as a result. This triad of 'authenticating' questions clarifies and brings full meaning to who you are as a total person, and creates a sound place from which to operate in pursuing and achieving career and life goals.

The Fourth Leg:

What Have I ACCOMPLISHED?

The things that fill your life today have roots in the past. Part of becoming more self-aware of our personal history involves looking at what we have done in our life. *This includes our accomplishments, achievements, experiences and the activities that gave us a sense of self-satisfaction.* There are achievements—in our career life and in our personal life that relate to families, friends and community—of which we feel proud. Achievements give us a sense of self-satisfaction that can be translated into other satisfying experiences. Personal achievements build on one another and can be used to support future endeavors.

The Fourth Leg question centers on how you have expanded your universe. Your answers will expose your proven strengths, forming a solid foundation, identifying who you are in terms of skills, talents, challenges and values. This question will also trigger thoughts and memories of situations where you did not achieve what you could have. As Tara recorded, the learning is in the doing. The situations where we fell short of what we were capable of should become instructive and show us how not to repeat the same mistakes, and give us a sense of where we must strive to improve.

The Six Legs process is all about helping you prepare to lead a more fulfilling life, and creating your own path to success. It's about building independence, increasing confidence, and identifying new "rules" for yourself. Your answers to the question *What have I ACCOMPLISHED?* will assist you in recognizing the value of your own package of individual talents, skills and options. Identifying what you have achieved in your life reinforces your confidence and stimulates thinking and reasoning power to open up more options, thus revitalizing your life. Knowledge has the power to guide you to new peaks of accomplishment.

How Do You Define an Accomplishment?

Accomplishments are the direct rewards deriving from the application of your tools, talents and skills. They culminate in a result. For example, your company increased its profit in the second quarter by x percent, you completed a big project on time and within budget, or you met specific sales objectives. Accomplishments are facts without feelings, and they come in various sizes, colors and shapes. Accomplishments often have a large people component to them. The people we're referring to could be those who were very much a part of our early upbringing and subsequent education, individuals in our workplace or people who have entered our life for a moment or for many years. They have been catalytic to our accomplishments. It could be a family member, a neighbor who gave you your first paycheck for mowing his lawn, or an encouraging teacher. It could be the first full-time job following graduation from college or university.

The demanding 'routine' of everyday life absorbs us so completely we often forget the significance of what was behind each of our accomplishments. This question brings us back to square one. Sometimes others see much more of what we have done than we do ourselves. If you don't believe that, just ask your spouse or a friend what they see as some of your accomplishments in the areas of work, life and as a human being. Self-awareness of other's opinions brings fluency to your skills, achievements and attitudes.

When we put together all of what we have now uncovered, we can not only identify but also clearly relate to our life's accomplishments. We should be optimistic about the road ahead. Each one of us is special and unique in our own right. The reflections at this time on the journey should enrich our lives and raise us to a level of excitement and, yes, passion. Is it worth the journey? The answer seems obvious.

Donna S. Vieira, editor of *Travel Bag*, used the traditional time of New Year's Day to look at her bin of data to visualize her future. In one of her editorials, she wrote:

> *In the past my resolutions usually meant giving up something I liked in my life rather than adding to it. This year I'm changing my approach. I'm doing more of what I like to do: Take time for myself. Take time to relax, to journal, or to meditate. Each week, review my values and make a date with someone I love. Then this fall take a personal retreat to review my goals, to read a book, to get clear about the life I truly want, and do the work of creating a wonderful life! Why settle for less?*

The lesson is simple. When we understand ourselves, we can understand and accept others more easily. Just ask Tara!

While the thought is still fresh in your mind, go to the A.C.T. Exercises at the end of this section and answer the Fourth Leg question (page 94).

C.

The Fifth Leg

How Did I CREATE What I Did?

This question centers on passion, commitment and competence. It spotlights the extent of your creativity and level of risk taking. What are the skills, values, talents, motivations or circumstances you have been aware of, made use of and applied throughout your life to create achievements? The skills and talents can be self-made or God-given. The sad fact of life is that we can get so caught up reacting to external demands and other people's agendas that it is entirely possible to journey through our years without exposing our God-given talents.

When you review your biography, it should become easy to begin listing the *hows* of your accomplishments which give support and credence to all you are and all you can be down the road. You have lots of good reasons to have pride in yourself. Tara's next question, *How did I CREATE what I did?* looks at the personal strengths and circumstances that energized her passion to perform and accomplish.

In examining how we have created the things we have, we are often struck with the realization that more things happen in an unplanned rather than a planned fashion. Creation jells when passion and commitment come together under the right circumstances—with a bit of serendipity and luck thrown in.

Using our natural strengths is an exhilarating experience. This is a vital piece of self-awareness. So often in our fast-changing world, our strengths are pushed to the back of our heads to the point where they are out of sight—and out of mind. Remembering how we created our accomplishments brings these strengths back to the forefront of our minds. The point is, once you know what your talents are, you seek out situations that allow you to use them.

The most critical ingredient in any accomplishment is the passion you display. Passion is the parent of commitment. To cite the importance of passion, we might want to consider the one area in all of our lives where we spend most of our time, namely our work. Having a clear passion for a field of work, a particular company or industry not only gets you the job, it *keeps* you in the job.

In the past, many believed you didn't need to be enthralled with the company or the industry if you were good at what you did. Today that is no longer good enough: employers reason that the only way a business will survive and prosper is if everyone involved believes that his or her willing contribution is critical.

Human resources firm Towers Perrin released a workplace study indicating that 40 percent of employees loathe their jobs. We would add that the underlying impact in these organizations is that employees will be working to a mere 30 percent of real capacity. Managers are stepping away from the theory that competence matters more than attitude. Bottom line is they are becoming convinced that genuine commitment or, if you will, passion is required of everyone. If you lack passion and commitment for what you do, you'll never achieve your full potential.

Many people we meet aren't in touch with how they feel about what they do for a living. They've given even less thought to the environment in which they'd like to work. In today's world you have to be emotionally intelligent. You have to possess a strong understanding of yourself and others. You can be brilliant at anything, but if you're unable to relate effectively with others, your days in the job may be numbered. We obtain a job interview because of our skills. We are offered the job because we're a good fit. We keep and develop in the job because we possess the interpersonal people skills to effectively work with others.

The *how did I CREATE?* question is meant to look below the surface of our life's accomplishments, to bring them into clearer view. As we examine the question, we realize that there were a number of influences and, particularly, people who were instrumental in helping us create what we did. These could be mentors at work or in our own families, teachers or people who nudged us to explore new interests or hobbies.

Take the example of a 40-year-old who, in conversation with friends, says "I really don't have mechanical skills," but is reminded by an old friend of the time, at age 11, when he and that good friend constructed a soapbox for entry in the local soapbox derby.

For those who have any experience in building a soapbox, there is a clear requirement for at least some mechanical ability, such as reading blueprints and using appropriate tools in the appropriate way. The individual's friend, who was shorter and lighter, was the one designated to ride the soapbox. At the end of the first heat, he crashed it. The crashing of the soapbox had nothing to do with the mechanical attributes of the soapbox. However, the crash had distorted the 40-year-old's memory of the experience, and caused him to lose sight of his own mechanical abilities. Upon reflection, he realized that he did, indeed, have some ability and had accomplished a significant goal—the building of a soapbox.

While the thought is still fresh in your mind, go to the A.C.T. Exercises at the end of this section and answer the Fifth Leg question (page 94).

T.

The Sixth Leg

What Were
My Personal TRIUMPHS?

Personal triumphs play to your passions and interests. Triumphs translate into living a bigger reality where the feelings behind what we did are as important as the facts. Triumphs are those things you achieve for yourself that elevate you beyond what you thought was possible. Picture this scenario: Your grand dream is to build your own sailboat and sail it around the world. Even though you've had no prior experience in building boats, you feel victorious even as you watch your boat take shape. Each step toward fulfilling your dream is a triumph in itself.

Triumphs impact your satisfaction and joy at a much deeper level than you could ever obtain if what you were doing was 'just a job.' To the outside world, completing your global voyage would be called an accomplishment, but to you it would be a tremendous personal triumph.

Our circumstance at a given moment may not offer us opportunity to pursue our interests. Often we find ourselves spending time on things we don't enjoy, whether it be at work or in other aspects of our life. We occupy life instead of living it.

When we reflect on what we consider to be the triumphs of our life, we are probing our skills and interests. This process makes us conscious that each of us, each individual among billions of people in the world, is absolutely unique. The problem with life's 'barnacle building' is that the unique 'me' gets pushed out of sight and way off the radar screen. But there's a one-of-a-kind person down there under those crustaceans. The effort to uncover the real you is worth its weight in gold. You can stand in awe when you take a look at this treasure trove. That's where you begin to understand the reasons why you are where you are at this moment.

Triumphs relate to our spirit. They are achievements that are in harmony with the passion and person we *really* are deep inside. They are goals you meet in your heart's best interest. When you look at your bin of data, where have you accomplished things that you consider triumphs of your spirit?

The following is a true story:
> *Randy and Jason were neighbors. They and their wives had always been great friends, and a couple of years ago they decided to buy houses next door to each other. Each Friday night after work, they would get together for a barbecue.*

One particular Friday evening while Jason was cooking the steaks, Randy blurted out, "Hey, Jas, did you hear about this songwriting contest they're promoting on the radio?"

"No ... why?" Jason responded.

"Well, I've been thinking about entering that contest," Randy replied.

"Why? You've never written songs before. It'll be a waste of time. Besides, to be a professional songwriter you have to pay your dues—be involved with the business, maybe start off as a musician, play for years in rundown, smoky bars," Jason scoffed.

Randy hesitated and digested the thought. "Well, I'm going to try it anyway." And he did. His song never made it to the contest. Instead, Randy took it directly to a publisher who liked what he heard. Within a year, radio stations were playing his material. If Randy had listened to the external logic, and not to his internal intelligence or gut feeling, his song might never have stirred the airwaves. To sum up with words attributed to comedian Jonathan Winters, "I couldn't wait for success so I had to go ahead without it."

Our pre-conceived belief system can be a formidable wall we have to surmount in order for a personal initiative or change to occur. We are continually rattled by 'mental rumors' and 'conscientious objectors' that whisper, "You can't expand beyond your safe boundaries of existing knowledge and skill." Sometimes we are so addicted to the old rules and ways that they obstruct our perceptions of our potential and ability to initiate change. We are bombarded with internal and external messages that tell us we'll fail for sure, so our first reactions are usually to ignore or deny change. This replays the old fears and insecurities, causing a mental melting away of our self-confidence. The resulting mental stress makes us vulnerable.

Following your heart takes courage. It puts you at risk. It's the fear of failure that makes you less than you deserve to be. Remember baseball idol Casey Stengel's offhanded remark: "You know they said it couldn't be done, but sometimes it doesn't always work out that way."

Once you've found your passion, pursuing it can take you beyond your normal comfort zone. If you are not committed to taking full ownership of its potential, it will live a small life.

Adding More Triumphs to Your Life

Triumphs are a celebration of yourself—you don't need a roaring crowd to recognize your victory. Your life is entirely of your own making; if you want to change your circumstances, you have to first change your thinking. Your mind creates your own reality. Negative thoughts have immense influence on the subconscious mind. If your subconscious has picked up worry and negativity, it will accept them as true and will work day and night feeding your thoughts to support your belief (I'll never get another job; I'm no good; He's right, I'll never be able to write a song...or negotiate these rapids...).

If you're not on guard, your subconscious will distort your perception of reality and stymie your impulse to try new things. You can change your perceptions by taking responsibility for your own reality. Challenge yourself to a mental scrubbing of all self-defeating beliefs, replacing them with positive thoughts (I'm a winner; I can accomplish anything). Repetition is the key. Strong and concentrated thoughts are strong and concentrated forces that will make the difference between success and failure. *Pay attention to the flow of thoughts streaming through your head.* New thoughts sparking out of your imagination are always looking for an outlet. A single, unaided thought hasn't much power. But the more often it's repeated, the more power and energy it generates. *What are some of the negative "beliefs" you'd like to scrub from your brain?*

I'm of Two Minds About That!

Let's say you like to analyze everything for supporting evidence before you'd even think of changing your mind about something. You would be classified as a dominant left-brain thinker. You'd tend to be logical, a gatherer and analyzer of information and a critical thinker. You're great at evaluating facts, figures and dates, making you shrewd by society's standards. Your life would be sensible, organized and on schedule.

Left-brain thinking has the ability to fall victim to rules and obligations and analysis paralysis. It likes to keep things as they are. It's the source of mental rumors (I'll never be able to change; I can't do that; That will never happen). Thinking on the left can be judgmental and close-minded; formulating its own interpretation of life and reality as being black or white; it wants rules for every contingency. A strong, dominant left-brain thinker loves routine, security and structure—and can be uncomfortable with change.

The left hemisphere operates and controls our daily lives, and focuses on our current state of affairs. This tends to limit our view of possibilities through the only thought system it knows, that of analytical and deductive reasoning. This forces us down a path of single-minded, sterile thinking. The left is so used to governing our life it has the tendency to jump in too quickly and throw cold water on a new idea before we've had time to play with it and polish it off. Nothing is more dangerous than an idea when it's the only one you have. It's like jumping out of an aircraft with no reserve parachute. The left's role is parent-like, attempting to keep us out of danger. It does have our best interests at heart, but if we're not careful, it can govern like a martinet and take all the fun out of life.

On the flip side, the right hemisphere is used for the purposes of breaking habits or existing patterns of thought and creating brand new possibilities to help us manage and cope with changes in our lives.

The right hemisphere rises from our spirit and likes to play with life's possibilities. We used it all the time when we were kids! It's where creativity, curiosity and imagination abound. It's the Disney world of our visual thoughts and dreams. It thinks about what is possible instead of what is not. The right is the side that is non-judgmental, childlike and free flowing. The right brain loves to change things and invent something new. It thrives on seeking new patterns through an open mind of different ideas, thoughts and actions. As we grew older, the rules and regulations that form the norms of society may have diminished the power of the right.

If we are ever to be in harmony with a changing world, we must develop a new set of thoughts, attitudes and actions. The answer lies in turning to the right side of our brains. We have to subdue judgmental thinking that extinguishes an idea before it has a chance to breathe life. We have to procure an open mind about what we can be and behold, so that life can be fun again.

Why Do Some People
Accomplish More Than Others?

True achievers augment and authenticate themselves by searching for their passions. Achievements driven by passion are triumphs of the spirit. Triumphs also deal with our *potential self*—the internal yearnings and dreamscapes we project for ourselves. We would all love to do what we do best and find our joy in doing it. Life is a continual process of improvement, reflection and refinement: a grindstone to either grind or hone us. It allows us to reinvent ourselves and adjust attitudes, values and beliefs we deem critical to our success. It's not what and where we are now, but who we can become in being all we can be. Triumphant moments stand out as peaks on our journey's lifeline.

Dreams come from the heart. Our spirit represents the divine energy in all of us. As we grow up, society begins to form our thoughts and push us in directions that distance us from the passion of our spirit. Triumphs of the spirit are pursued by an inner drive that moves ahead without considering the fact that we may lack the skills, talent or education to even attempt them. The expertise is found in the doing. Our skills and talents are honed in the process. Triumphs are the success of the spirit. They have great power to change belief systems and highlight the vital potential within each of us.

When comedian Bill Cosby was asked for his defi-
nition of success, he responded, "I don't know what
success is, but I know the definition of failure is
trying to please everybody."

While the thought is still fresh in your mind, go to the A.C.T. Exercises at the end of this section and answer the Sixth Leg question (page 94).

A.C.T. Exercises: The DOING Part of You

Destination: adding greater meaning and clarity to your uniqueness

The Fourth Leg: What did I ACCOMPLISH?

Start out with a blank sheet of paper. List your accomplishments. What do you bring to the table? Often we don't give ourselves enough credit for how creative we are. What have others appreciated about us?

The Fifth Leg: How did I CREATE my accomplishments?

When you answer this question, concentrate on your passions, commitments and competencies.

The Sixth Leg: What were my personal TRIUMPHS?

This question centers on the inner you, your spirit-directed triumphs. Think about those times you felt wonderful about what you were doing. Did others share your joy and excitement?

Afterthought...

How will this bin of data influence the action plans you pre-
pared in the Multiple Me exercise (see page 64).

Tara's Journey

*Following our path is in effect a kind of going off the path,
through open country; there is a certain early stage when we
are left to camp out in the wilderness, alone, with few supporting voices. Out there in the silence we must build a hearth,
gather the twigs and strike the flint for the fire ourselves. If we
can see the path laid out for us, there is a good chance it is
not our path: it is probably someone else's we have substituted
for our own. Our own path must be deciphered every step of
the way.*

—David Whyte

The river Tara rafted on in the northern wilderness has
many stories and doesn't give up its history easily. Many
people had taken the journey before her. Long ago it was
a corridor for fur traders to get them from one place to
another in building the country's future. But to Tara, it
became a ribbon of water transporting and submerging
her into the riches that lay beneath the surface of her
life. As water touched land, the land touched her inner
nature.

The secret of learning a subject in depth is to write about it. Tara's process of writing a biography of *uncovery* created a reference library that encompassed her whole being. It was a process of quickening self-awareness—a guiding light shining on untrodden paths. Her biography worked as a filter. It had her pay attention to her experiences, letting them rise to the surface so she could draw meaning and learning from them, while clarifying and adding meaning to her life. It changed the perception she had of herself. The real learning happened inside the interactions and circumstances of her life. In her 'islands of silence' she became more aware of the strengths and 'silent victories' within her history.

There are aspects of Tara in each of us. She captures the reality of life today and the need to get away from it all to take stock of your life. The act of writing your biography submerges you into your subconscious, which is far more intelligent than your conscious mind. The subconscious is the gateway to processing your life experience, interacting with your spirit, acknowledging your strengths, skills and accomplishments, and accessing personal wisdom. It has a direct line into your intuition which is attached to your soul, the blueprint of your true personality.

We carry with us everything we do in life. The art of life is to look over our shoulder and learn from those experiences. Take time to reflect, absorb and ponder where you've been and the investment you've put into your life. The knowledge you find there is the essence of your inner spirit. Listen to your spirit, and trust the voice of your experience.

Human nature has a limited tolerance for change, and most of us are more comfortable when we live a life of predictability. Change will always be a reality of life. Many of us can take comfort in the words of the 45-year-old who says, "I believe that I am more vital and alive now than at any other time of my life. My transitions were more useful to my journey than I had wanted to believe while I was in the midst of them."

The Six-Legged Stool

Through her restored self-understanding, Tara clarified and validated that she was truly the Alpha being in her life. The last powerful act of her trip was to document in her Alpha Log her commitment to pursue only those things that would make her happy and restore her sense of balance.

Tara brought her six carved branches back to Manhattan. In her mind, she could readily visualize them as the six legs of a stool. She viewed the stool as a metaphor. In essence, the seat was supported by the strength of her accumulated history and the self-awareness and confidence about who she was, what she had become and why. The six-legged stool was a source of pride, authenticated knowledge and inner confidence upon which she could stand or sit at any time to meet the challenges in her personal and business life.

Tara returned to work with a new attitude and openness. When Tara was asked, "How is it going?" She replied, "I'm working on wonderful."

Brent Habig, founder and CEO of Tigris Consulting in New York City, was quoted in a business magazine as saying, "acting confident when you don't feel that way is a complicated risk that's best avoided. If your confidence isn't based in the knowledge that you can deliver, you risk letting people down." You also risk letting yourself down.

Success results from a combination of experience, choices, talent, people, external factors, luck and opportunity. The Six Legs process peels the layers off your history to have you pay attention to, and learn the appropriate lessons from, your life's successes and fumbles. It gives legitimacy to your own thinking about the dimensions and possibilities within yourself so you can move ahead and live a more peaceful life grounded in a sound and strong sense of your potential.

Without Confidence, Nothing Happens

Confidence is synonymous with preparation and is about one thing: clarity. The Six Leg's requirement that you write your biography instills within you a confidence that is rooted in your internal truth which you can pull from your mental drawers at any time. It's the difference between trying to live up to a false confidence—which is a serious misreading of your ability—and the real confidence that is validated through the documentation of your experiences and learning.

Chris Carmichael, founder and chairman of Carmichael Training Systems in Colorado Springs, commented in *INC* magazine: "Both champion athletes and CEOs are good at mentally drawing upon their past successes to step into uncharted territory. When I'm working with an athlete, I'll have them do a mental recall of what they've accomplished. If you do it right the athlete starts to swell with confidence."

You'll find your 'bin of data' has a pervasive presence that becomes a positive and respected source of strength. It brings forward all those things that make up the real you. The information was always there—in truth, you knew it all along—but you weren't really aware of its significance. If you've truly put your heart into the process of uncovering your bin of data, you'll never *un*know what you've found there. Your new self-awareness will infuse itself into everything you do from now on, and enrich your thinking, attitude, confidence, choices and relationships, be they in the world of work, family or community.

The mind, once expanded to the dimensions of larger ideas, never returns to its original size.

— Oliver Wendell Holmes

One evening while walking with a friend on 42nd Street in Manhattan, Tara heard jazz music drifting out of a club located in the basement of a building. The music pulled her in. Little did she know this would be a defining moment in her life. Tara loved what she heard and how it made her feel. The environment spoke to her inner being.

Within a year, Tara had left Quor Power International and opened **Six Legs Jazz Club** in Bass Harbor, Maine. The entrance stood only 50 yards from the liberating waves of the Atlantic Ocean.

All the stools in her bar had six legs.

Jazzed Up!

Are you looking to find the 'jazz' in your life? The musical harmony in jazz comes from a hidden construction and discipline that forces you to listen to the silence between the notes.

As you open your mind to what you have learned while engaging in the Six Legs process, you'll begin to feel the jazz in your life. You will be able to move in the direction that will put you in harmony with your nature.

You could spend your whole life searching for your inner truth, but in the end it will find you if you are open to the experience of uncovery. Tara found this to be true. When she gave in to her real self, life became clearer and lighter.

Thoughtwork Exercise:
Writing the WONDERFUL into your future

Destination: to blueprint the future
life goals that contain your passion

Instructions: What is your spirit really after? Find a quiet
spot or activity that allows you to relax and set your imagination free. Take yourself to the 35,000-foot level and become
an observer of your future horizons.

Your future is unwritten…this is your opportunity to author
your own destiny. This is a no-risk exercise. *Over the next 10
years, what personal accomplishments and triumphs, driven
by your passion and spirit, would you want included in your
biography? What would you start working on tomorrow if you
had absolutely no chance of failing?*

List them in your journal. Don't get fixated by the numbers;
just get caught up in the thought game.

Appendix A

ChangeActions for Success

Is There a Formula for Success?

Don Hewitt, originator and executive producer of the highly rated television program *60 Minutes*, stated: "I don't know the formula for success, but I know the formula for failure—it's sitting on your laurels." The point is, you have to continually move ahead in life, or have your options wither away before your eyes. Continually nurture your ability to experience the joy of learning and build your powers of understanding and perception.

Individuals who are successful at embracing change share some common characteristics. They actively manage the information that's injected into their brain. They constantly challenge conventional wisdom by looking for opportunities to stimulate a dynamic exchange of ideas. They subscribe to flexible learning and unanticipated discoveries based on serendipitous events. They allow a thinking attitude that opens them up to trying new things on an experimental basis just to see where they lead. They become involved in their own thinking, favoring reflection over immediate action. They take time to internalize their own thoughts and feelings in order to comprehend what's going on and how it affects them. They focus on anticipating what happens next before it happens. They network extensively.

What you think and do today is indispensably important to how you live tomorrow. The following are some specific actions you need to execute on a regular basis if you want to live up to your potential. We call these *ChangeActions*.

ChangeAction #1

Take Time to Hear Yourself Think

Pierre Elliot Trudeau, former prime minister of Canada, had a lifelong passion for canoeing. He stated in his memoirs: "I think a lot of people want to go back to basics sometimes to find their bearings. For me a good way is to get back to nature by canoe. Canoeing forces you to make a distinction between your needs and your wants. You deal with who you are and what you're doing. Then let nature fill in the void. You discover a sort of simplifying of your values, a distinction between values artificially created and those that are necessary for your spiritual and human development." Go paddle your own "transition canoe."

In planning what's best for you, you have to go back to basics. Make the effort to eliminate the clutter and noise from your life and get close to your thoughts and feelings about what's important to you. Inner feelings let you connect deeply with yourself. They are your drivers—if you don't feel, you don't know who or what you are.

ChangeAction #2

Anticipate Your Antiquity

In the movie *Dead Poets Society*, Robin Williams, in his role as Mr. Keating, a teacher at a private school, told his class of young men:

> *They're not that different from you, are they? Same haircuts. Full of hormones, just like you. Invincible, just like you feel. The world is their oyster. They believe they're destined for great things, just like many of you. Their eyes are full of hope, just like you. Did they wait until it was too late to make from their lives even one iota of what they were capable? Because you see gentlmen, these boys are now fertilizing daffodils. But if you listen real close, you can hear them whisper their legacy to you. Go on, lean in. Carpe. Hear it? Carpe. Carpe Diem. Seize the day boys, make your lives extraordinary.*

You only have so much time allotted to you in life. Don't waste it. Make the best of it. *Carpe diem*. Seize the day!

ChangeAction #3

Create a Learning Crisis

No change = no growth.

Take a walk on the wild side, step out of your comfort zone and create a change crisis of new learning and growth for yourself. An extreme change crisis pushes you to the breaking point where you have to dig down inside yourself in order to overcome and survive. The act of doing so allows you to grow, and gives you a clearer perspective of what you're really capable of doing. The credo of the Outward Bound organization is to strive and to not yield. Their trips to the wilderness pit you against the elements of nature to transport you beyond your fears. The action of releasing your fear is an exhilarating human experience. Your emotions are pushed to the limits. But through it all you've learned to survive, to know yourself more completely and confidently.

Why not create a stimulating personal adventure of your own to take you beyond the perceptions of your own reality? Set a schedule now. Have you tried parachuting or wild river rafting, taking piano lessons, writing a book, or canoeing in the wilderness? Try something different; you'll never be the same.

ChangeAction #4

Rent a "Change Attitude"

Insanity is doing the same thing endlessly. A professional adventurer and Arctic explorer was asked if he'd walk the grueling trek across the Bering Strait a second time. His answer: "No, life is too short to do the same thing twice."

Human nature makes it doubtful that we'll ever open up our minds to other discoveries unless we can prove conclusively (left-brain logic) that it is worthwhile. So over the next month, rent an attitude to change your life in little ways. Give yourself permission to experiment with small daily, safe changes in your life (take an alternate route to work, eat different food, take sugar in your coffee, go to the opera, take your parking attendant to lunch). Aim for something that makes you feel good; better yet, it should be FUN. Small changes have a big payback in inspiring you to make bigger ones. They provide an environment that enables you to allow things to happen in a more challenging way.

Singer/songwriter Billy Joel commented in an interview, "I attempt to try songwriting every day, even if I don't feel like it. Because suddenly a great possibility pops up just by fooling around."

Every day holds a fresh promise made just for you.

ChangeAction #5

Intellectualize Your Day

Take your "vitamin C." Be CURIOUS, for heaven's sake!
Turn each and every day into a meaningful experience. To the
Japanese, simply doing things is meaningless unless one is able
to become deeper and wiser along the way.

Look back on the events of your day to review what happened.
Mentally debate what you've learned, how you've felt and why.
If you don't let your feelings rise to the surface, you won't
plumb the depth of understanding of who you are and what
you are capable of doing. Discern in what way you are wiser
today than yesterday. It's a simple but insightful exercise.

ChangeAction #6

Nurture Worldly Wisdom

Facts and information are indispensable to our lives. But there
is little time to internalize, comprehend and synthesize completely the enormous amount of information being thrown at
us today. The new rule directs us to filter the information coming into our brain and to weed out the clutter. We have to
delve into the facts that are important to us and develop a
deeper perspective on those issues that affect our life (religion,
education, crime, abortion, gun control, the environment...).

We have to wise up and be more conversant and knowledge-able on current events.

Think globally. Look at the new economic hot spots evolving in the world. Find out where we're all heading. One means of doing this is to fire up a file folder on the topics that interest you. Your files are timesavers and information storage bays; skimming over an article that you have filed is like calling on a mentor, as the written word can spark new ways of thinking. Bottom line, be and stay informed.

From there, accumulate everyday research by clue-clipping magazine and newspaper articles on topics for further digestion (don't forget the scrap paper and pen to capture comments you hear during the day). Mentally debate the pros and cons you have on topics to formulate a considered opinion of your own. Look for opportunities to discuss the issues with your friends and associates to garner their wisdom and crystallize your thinking. After a while you'll start to feel more in control of the information and your knowledge on a wide variety of subjects.

ChangeAction #7

Ask Engaging Questions

The secret of a great conversationalist is asking great ques-tions. Engaging questions are important stimuli to the mind. Questions are used to "Q up" your desire to know. They snap your mind to attention and act as steroids to the brain; they are the most powerful source of new knowledge. Questions probe the mind, break old habits and open the doors of learning, insight and thoughtful action. Engaging questions are the intellectual nutrients in the development of reasoning power and intuition. They are the main gateway through which floods new learning and more questions. Enough said?

ChangeAction #8

Be a Bookworm

Reading an assortment of books and magazines opens up the theater of the mind. It's a great escape, as well as an awesome means to learn and gain a wider perspective on the world. Reading puts you in the company of authors. Join a book club for a year.

You will discover thoughts and opinions you never knew you had, and gain a better command of language.

Extensive reading serves to organize your thought patterns and make you a better communicator. It will broaden your horizons, heighten your curiosity about the unfamiliar, and present an outside perspective on a different topic, interest or area of life.

ChangeAction #9

Improve Perceptive Powers

Under the old rules, we never really gave much thought to the future being unpredictable. Time unraveled at a more leisurely pace, giving us breathing room to adjust our plans to conform with the unfolding future.

These days, tomorrow is coming at us in fast forward. Not being able to perceive what's happening next causes us all kinds of grief and turmoil. Part of gaining control involves improving our perceptive skills in order to "see" the future coming. Increased perception prepares us for what is about to happen. Nobody can predict fully all that will happen tomorrow. But anyone who stays tuned to news stories on television, radio and in newspapers and magazines, and keeps their ear to the ground with friends and business associates, can improve the *probability factor* of their predictions. Knowing a little something does wonders for your comfort zone.

How often do you use your intuition to make decisions? Think of your intuition as a normal part of daily living. You can encourage your intuitive sense by telling your subconscious mind to be receptive to your intuition. Practice making some intuitive decisions of your own, even on insignificant things (for example, while you are grocery shopping, predict the amount of the food bill as you get to the cashier). Above all, continue to be positive. This attitude takes practice. Keep reminding yourself that you are becoming better at it everyday. For a great book on intuition, pick up *GUTFEELING* by Peter Urs Bender.

ChangeAction #10

Have Fun!

Liven up your day. Take time to play—go fly a kite! Nourish your sense of humor; put more fun and laughter into your life. Keep a weekly log (you can use a picture album) to record the things you do for fun.

Appendix B

Wise Words

on Life, Learning and Change

The paths to the future are not found but made, and the activity of making them changes both the maker and the destination.

John Scharr

Success seems to be connected with action. Successful people keep moving. They make mistakes but they don't quit.

Conrad Hilton

Eat one live toad in the morning and nothing worse will happen to you the rest of the day.

Jack Handey

If I had eight hours to chop down a tree, I'd spend six of them sharpening my axe.

Abraham Lincoln

Until you make peace with who you are, you'll never be content with what you have.

Doris Mortman

Most of the time I don't have fun, and the rest of the time I don't have any fun at all.

Woody Allen

Everything you do in life prepares you for what you're going to end up doing.

Mike Bullard

In a world that is constantly changing, there is no one subject or set of subjects that will serve you in the foreseeable future, let alone for the rest of your life. The most important skill to acquire now is learning how to learn.

John Naisbitt

Old Dakota tribal saying: When you're riding a dead horse the best strategy is to dismount.

I've learned that only through focus can you do world-class things, no matter how capable you are.

Bill Gates

The people who get on in this world are the people who get up and look for the circumstances they want, and if they can't find them, make them.

George Bernard Shaw

You are the product of your imagination. You are as mighty, as weak, or as capable as you think you are.

Mohammad Ali

Sit at the feet of your own life and be taught by it!

Polly Berends

Appendix C

Things Worth Knowing

Alpha is all about leadership...taking back control, finding our own territory and becoming our own leader.

Here are some things worth knowing as you assume the leadership of your life.

❖ The value of time

❖ The obligation of duty

❖ The success of perseverance

❖ The wisdom of economy

❖ The pleasure of working

❖ The virtue of patience

❖ The dignity of simplicity

❖ The improvement of talent

❖ The power of kindness

❖ The joy of originating

❖ The influence of example

❖ The possibilities of life

The Authors

Dick Cappon

Prior to his current role as founder and president of Cappon Associates, Dick was a partner and senior principal in two of Canada's major accounting and consulting practices. He held the position of National Personnel Partner with Coopers & Lybrand (now PricewaterhouseCoopers), and as a senior principal, led the career transition practice in the greater Toronto area for Ernst & Young. During his tenure with Coopers & Lybrand, he chaired the International Personnel Committee, during which time he traveled throughout Europe, Africa, South America, the United Kingdom and the U.S. Dick has also held the position of Canadian vice-president for Drake Beam Morin.

Dick is a published author with numerous articles to his credit on the many dimensions of career planning, focusing on the action steps that maximize an individual's unique talents and qualities. He is sought-after as a guest speaker in the area of career planning and management by a diverse group of business and community organizations. The *Toronto Star* invited Dick to write a series of articles on the career implications in our ever-changing world of work. In 1992, the Cablenet TV channel in Oakville, Ontario, awarded him the Education Award for its *Lunchtime Live* series. In 1995 Dick received its Award of Excellence for the same show. He has a record of extensive community service. A pinnacle of recognition came when he received the "Paul Harris Fellow" designation from the Rotary Foundation of Rotary International. A lifetime devotee of physical fitness, Dick completed his fifth marathon in Toronto in September 2003.

Dick earned a B.Sc. in Social Science from St. John Fisher College, Rochester, New York and has attended numerous management development programs. He completed the Advanced Management Program, Beaumont School of Management, University of Denver, and is certified in Alternate Dispute Resolution, University of Windsor, Faculty of Law.

Dick has numerous professional affiliations, including election as the first president of the Canadian Chapter of the International Association of Career Management Professionals (IACMP). In 1999, the IACMP Toronto chapter elected him to its Hall of Fame. Dick is co-founder of a Toronto-based coaching consortium, a network of international coaches and a member of the International Coach Federation (ICF). He resides in Oakville, Ontario.

John R. Christensen

John is president of Mind Sharing
Consulting Services Inc.,
a business mentoring and personal
coaching firm. Formerly, John was one
of the architects and builders of a
groundbreaking corporate management

institute for one of Canada's major banks. John's experience
has also encompassed senior management roles in marketing,
credit card product management, corporate turnaround situations and restructuring initiatives. He has contributed as a
member on advisory committees mentoring the development of
entrepreneurial companies. John
has a reputation of being a thought-leader in the coaching
field. He has authored and published a cutting-edge coaching
process called the Co-Pilot Professional Coaching System.
Co-Pilot provides a disciplined framework to unlock and
develop the potential in others. The system is used by professional coaches in the U.S., Canada and Europe.

As an energized presenter, workshop facilitator and program
developer, John brings over three decades of experience and

education to corporations in addressing their needs in the areas of relationship management, team collaboration and leadership development. A representative list of his coaching clientele include the senior executive ranks of banking and financial institutions, manufacturing industries, legal and technology companies, as well as career management firms.

John lives life with curiosity. On one sabbatical, he drove an eighteen-wheeler around North America for seven months. He wrote about the experience and was published as a feature article, "Hell on Wheels...from the executive suite to the cab of a big rig, one man's journey," in *London Business Magazine*. John is the author of the self-discovery journal Releasing the *Human Kite Within*, along with numerous programs on self-development. He is a published lyricist for RCA and Polydor records and an entrepreneur several times over.

His eclectic educational background includes a stint at York University in Humanities, Cow/Calf Management and Crop Nutrition from the University of Guelph, Artificial Insemination accreditation from the American Breeders Association, as well as numerous management programs. John is a member of the International Coach Federation (ICF), The World Future Society and co-founder of a Toronto-based coaching consortium, a network of international coaches. John resides in Burlington, Ontario.

Your Feedback

We would like to know what greater meaning and clarity this book has brought to your life and how you might have changed because of it. We welcome your feedback.

If you'd like more information on any of the ideas and challenges presented here, or would like to arrange speaking engagements or workshops based on the Six Legs process, simply contact us using the information below:

Dick Cappon: coachcappon@yahoo.com

John R. Christensen: jchristensen@sympatico.ca

Did you enjoy
Six Legs Jazz Club?

Would you like to share it with
someone you care about?

To order additional copies, please contact:
Creative Bound Inc.
at (613) 831-3641
or 1-800-287-8610
(toll-free North America)
orderdesk@creativebound.com
www.creativebound.com

Organizations, businesses and retailers—
ask about our wholesale discounts for
multiple-copy orders!